ISBN 978-88-6242-287-1

First Italian edition September 2018

Photo credits:
Gyoun Nam 14-15
Susan Wides 10, 32, 34, 35
Diana Carta 28-29
Paul Warchol 4, 52-53, 56, 64, 66, 67, 68-69, 70, 71, 72-73

Cover photo credit: © Iwan Baan
Book design: Martina Distefano
Proofreading: Richard Lisle

LetteraVentidue Edizioni S.r.l.
Corso Umberto I, 106
96100 Siracusa, Italy

Web: www.letteraventidue.com
Facebook: LetteraVentidue Edizioni
Twitter: @letteraventidue
Instagram: letteraventidue_edizioni

DIANA CARTA

LAKE OF
THE MIND

A CONVERSATION WITH

STEVEN
HOLL

LetteraVentidue

CONTENTS

YEHUDA E. SAFRAN

INTRODUCTION

I met Steven Holl more than 20 years ago at a Paola Iacucci project review. He turned to me and said: "You remind me of somebody I knew" I said "I hope a nice man" he replied, "Yes, very nice, Alvin Boyarsky".
It turned out that it was Alvin who invited him to the Architectural Association and made him assistant to Rem Koolhaas while Zaha Hadid was a student at their Unit. It was Alvin, following my Adolf Loos exhibition at the ICA in London (1985), who appointed me in charge of Theory and the Diploma Thesis at the AA. Steven then went on to invite me to his own review the following day. It was dominated by a debate on the analogical versus the digital. We ended up, as many reviews do, in an Italian restaurant.
At the time I was living in Rome, but, when at the end of the dinner Steven turned to me and asked me if I would care to join him at the GSAPP at Columbia University the

following semester, I replied that I would be happy to do so. Indeed, in that September of 1996, I began working at the school running an Advanced Studio with Steven and joined him at the office for Pin Ups.

What have I learned about his *modus operandi* in these years? If as the Dutch psychologist and historian J.H. van den Berg claimed that all painters are born Phenomenologists: "Objects have something to say to us -this is common knowledge among poets and painters. Therefore, poets and painters are born phenomenologists. Or rather, we are all born phenomenologists; the poets and painters among us, however, are capable of conveying their views to others, a procedure also attempted laboriously, by the professional phenomenologist. We all understand the language of objects".

Then of course this does equally, or above all, apply to architects.

Reality cannot be taken for granted. Suspending our belief in the existence of the world, we are thrown again and again on to our primacy of perception. We see the world differently every time we close our eyes and open them again. If you add the constructions in our mind, you end up with infinite versions, which constitute the reality in which we live with one perspective version competing with another. Each connected in a web of conceptual tissues of assumptions. Or as Max Weber put it so memorably: "It is as if mankind is nothing but an insect immersed in a tissue of assumptions he himself has spun".

Perhaps the sharp contrast between the environment Steven was exposed to in his youth, his sojourn in Rome, and the graduation from Seattle, did the trick and threw him into the life of endless exploration, which became his life.

The absolute autonomy once gained in one's dream and nowhere else, became dominant in his creative life. Hence, his dedication to watercolour during every morning of his life in which the reality of the dream still persists before the onslaught of the daily tasks is mingled with the pristine state of the dream reality.

It was by pure chance that Steven was sitting next to a Canadian philosopher on the transcontinental Canadian train; a philosopher specialized in Maurice Merleau-Ponty. Steven was halfway there already, thanks to his intuition, but this encounter brought the needed concepts into his reach.

It reinforced his conviction that whatever he felt and perceived was of immense importance and value.

As Immanuel Kant observed: "Intuition without concept is blind, concept without intuition is empty".

It was not the purely conceptual phenomenology of Edmund Husserl, but the radical empiricism of Maurice Merleau-Ponty's Phenomenology of Perception and the Primacy of Perception, not to speak of The Visible and the Invisible from which Steven acquired the term *Kiasma*, the finish version of *Chiasma*, a title of a chapter in "The Visible and the Invisible".

Largely, it gave him the courage of his conviction that our reality is highly malleable and elastic. We are the authors of what we consider our reality.

Indeed, it facilitates his own tuning to the voices within.

He developed an acute sense of patterns in time. It came to him from poetry and music. Few, if any, matched his ability to turn the musical composition of musicians such as Béla Bartók and Morton Feldman to patterns in space.

Above all, to be able to conjugate external input from the world with the inner sensibilities of form.

Almost a Platonic textbook where the form is an ideal.

The wildest aquarelles are transformed again and again.

The transformation of any material to architecture is Steven Holl's greatest talent and ability. Not without a measure of cunning which makes the impossible possible and buildable.

If you take for example the Knut Hamson House and you observe with what wit and humor Steven transformed a scene from the Danish film *Hunger* into the balcony with yellow glass in the project you acquire an insight into his *modus operandi*.

Of course, there are countless examples of this nature but in this case, this note will be transformed into something other than a mere introduction to Diana Carta's illuminating interview.

OVERLOOKING 31ST STREET IN MIDTOWN WEST IN NEW YORK CITY, STEVEN HOLL RECOUNTS HOW HIS CREATIVE PROCESS ORIGINATES AND DEVELOPS THROUGH A PARTICULAR STYLE OF WORKING, LEADING TO WHAT CHARACTERIZES HIS FORM OF ARCHITECTURE.

IT IS THROUGH A DESCRIPTION
OF HIS LATEST PROJECTS
THAT THE ARCHITECT WILL
ILLUSTRATE THE TOOLS OF
HIS WORK AND THE PLACE
WHERE THIS IS CONCEIVED
AND CONTEMPLATED: "THE
CREATIVE WORK BEGINS IN THE
SOLITUDE OF THE CONNECTION
OF THE MIND/HAND/EYE. THE
SOLITARY ROOM WITH A TABLE
AND A CHAIR IS A FUNCTIONAL
DRAWING STUDIO"*

*STEVEN HOLL, BLACK SWAN THEORY, PRINCETON
ARCHITECTURAL PRESS, MARCH 2007, P. 151.

DIANA CARTA

A CONVERSATION WITH STEVEN HOLL

DIANA CARTA Whenever one has the opportunity to meet the most influential artists and architects you try not only to learn from their work but also to gain an insight into the mindset and working practices, understanding how the creative process originates and develops through a particular style of working.
Since time immemorial researchers and thinkers have been interested and fascinated by the topic: how the creative process develops and what influences the creativity that leads to the final result of the synthesis. On this occasion I would like to discuss those subjects with you, about the place where you work and the importance of the *genius loci*, not only in relation to the resulting buildings, but also in relation to the space where they were designed and developed.
In effect, it is fascinating to see how artists and architects choose their studios with care as these exert an

incredibly important influence on their work and their artistic creations.

As a result, the place where the work is done is often a determining factor. Various examples immediately spring to mind, such as Le Corbusier, who had a studio for painting that was separate from the one he used for architecture. It was a place he was very fond of, on the seventh and eighth floors of a building in the Porte Molitor district of Paris. He went there every morning, painted for hours and displayed his large paintings in a room with walls of exposed brick. Although he also loved working in his cabin, a small studio-house facing the sea in Cap-Martin in the south of France.

There is also the particular example of Mondrian's studio, where there is a strong sense of connection between his work and the place where it was created: being there means experiencing and perceiving the meaning of the compositions of the paintings.

Furthermore, an unusual case is Álvaro Siza, who goes to cafés to work on his architecture. These public places seem to create the ideal conditions to spark his creativity.

After this general introduction, I would like to talk with you about this topic, because in your case it seems to take on an even stronger meaning.

As it is known, your architecture is not approachable through the medium of a "Style" and your buildings being almost intrinsic to the situation, the site and the program, the *genius loci* plays a crucial role. It is a key element, among the complexity of the events, phenomena and ideas, which generates the spatial intuition of the designed project.

Following on from this, can you please tell me how you relate to the place where you work, and in particular to your small studio, the Round Lake Hut?

STEVEN HOLL The actual site of contemplation is really this five-by-seven-inch watercolour. I have been doing this for over thirty years: the first sketch, the first concept sketch, of every building we have done starts here. I use this format because it allows me to work anywhere, even on an aeroplane tray during my travels in the Unites States and China. I always have my watercolour paints with me. When there isn't much room, I still can have my paints and a little water on the side and I can work on my drawings. So this is actually the site, these 5 by 7 inches and, as you can see, there are 20,000 here, filed in the studio. I do have a watercolour desk in my apartment, in the Village, which has everything I need, but my favourite place is here, painting at the edge of the lake, in the Round Lake Hut. This is an ideal place. This way of working gives me complete and absolute clarity about what I'm doing.
It puts everything in chronological order and as I am working on a project I can see what came first and what is going on and where it is going.
Sometimes there are different projects underway at the same time; we have nine things under construction right now, so I have to develop the details for each of these buildings. By keeping everything on record, I can remember various things and by going back to my pad I can find them in the file, because it's all chronological. So, there is a certain rigor to the format. I also believe that it is important to study the programme, analizing all the aspects and visiting the

FROM ANCIENT CHINA TO GREECE

STEVEN HOLL - WATERCOLOURS

site; but you can't predict when the actual creative idea is going to occur. So, my method is to get up and draw, first thing in the morning, before eating breakfast or talking to anyone. I have some green tea and I postpone reading the news for later in the day, in order not to ruin the poetry of the moment. Then I work for one or two hours on my paintings; they're not always necessarily about the project. In other words, by being totally free, I can accidentally stumble on something that could be the project. I love this sort of half-awake, half-asleep moment, when I wake up from my dreams – it is total freedom.

That is really important to me, because I think that intuition and pragmatic thought have to be mixed to get a creative thought. Intuition is totally subjective, whereas pragmatic thought is objective, that's the fact, and it concerns all those aspects related to the site, to the dimensions and to other different circumstances: how big it is, where it is, which way it is facing, what is the site and so on. But the true creative thought only comes when it is mixed with some subjective feelings, which is not something that you can describe in words *a priori*. It appears and I am not actually sure where it comes from but it appears and suddenly you can begin to work with this intuition.

That is the reason why we made a video called "Drawing as thought", which is another important thing for me: drawing is a form of thought.

The project is not a complete thought, but it can be a form of thought to get out with words and then it becomes something that can drive a design. I don't have any words for that, but that is a thought.

It is an indefinite, indeterminate and aleatory process within the mind portion of the brain. Thoughtful architecture can begin with a new openness in stochastic and analogical thinking.

Stochastic thinking sets creative work in a state of suspense and it is central to the imaginative, creative act. It cannot be pre-determined; unlike scientific and rational thought. Between the false boundaries of architecture, sculpture, painting and music, there exists a blurred zone of exciting potential, where the indeterminate beginning is pregnant with imaginational force. Analogical thinking is an intertwining of the interworking of architecture and all of the arts. Like an ecosystem interjoining, the symbiosis is the nature of the arts and architecture can be a new open correlation in the 21st century, when now we are finally free of dogmatic theories of rationalism, postmodernism and deconstruction. Curiosity, imagination and enthusiasm hold a power in the mind to ignite the creative act. In clouds of automatic action, the unknowing create; aims swirl as thoughts start. Intuition is blowing as the joy of making any art expands.

The most pleasant place to do this is of course in absolute silence, in the Round Lake Hut, all away from noises like these around us now: constant construction noises, sirens or anything like that.

DC This is one of the aspects I wanted to cover with you, regarding in fact the diversity of your work places: one in the center of the dynamic and noisy City of New York and the other in the silence and the solitude of the countryside.

Consequently, could you tell me in what way you relate

to these two very different locations and how your work also relates to them?

SH It is good having both places, one in the city and one in the countryside. Either way, this office space is not enough.

It started almost twenty years ago, when I was working in a little loft in Manhattan. It was hot and I couldn't sleep because of the sound of the air conditioner so I decided to buy this little stone house in Rhinebeck with four acres around it and access to the Round Pound Lake. I started to go there in the summer on Fridays and to come back on Mondays. It is a great place to work and the lake is one of the highest in Dutchess County – it is all spring-fed water and provides beautiful swimming.

Then around six years after I arrived, I decided to build this hut close to the lake, with a wood structure and two glass elevations. It is so small, at just 80 square feet, that it doesn't count as a building, which meant it could be located as close as possible to the lake. It doesn't have foundations, electricity or water; it is so small that my body heat can heat it up. In the winter I can actually work in it; there could be snow outside on the ground but the sun shines through the skylight and I can work in a coat. In the summer, it is perfect – there is absolute silence and I can concentrate.

DC There is a particular detail of the Round Lake Hut that I would like to linger on: the small window only 1 foot x4 feet in the lower part of the wall and facing the light of the sunrise. How important is this moment of day with regard to how you work?

ROUND LAKE HUT

SH It allows me to sleep there if I want and to wake up with the sun.

DC So, can it be considered as a sort of celebration of that moment of the day?

SH I always wake up at dawn. No matter where I am, whether it's in New York or China. When dawn breaks, I wake up and I work in absolute silence and solitude.

DC This reminds me of the words you used to describe the Round Lake Hut: "The creative work begins in the solitude of the connection of the mind/hand/eye. The solitary room with a table and a chair is a functional drawing studio".

1. STEVEN HOLL, BLACK SWAN THEORY, PRINCETON ARCHITECTURAL PRESS, MARCH 2007, P. 151

SH Exactly, It's like a Zen meditation in the morning.

DC Was the presence of the lake another element that led you to choose this place? The map shows that it covers almost the whole area of the property. Furthermore, I have read that your family has Norwegian origins and the landscape in some way recalls that country's large lakes and woods.

SH The lake, or better the water's horizon, is something I grew up with in Puget Sound, Seattle; the landscape is characterized by the presence of a very large body of water. It has a very Scandinavian look. When the sun rises, you have this incredible condition of light on a horizontal body of water. As you know, the tide goes in and out following the cycle of the

ROUND LAKE HUT

moon, which is also connected to your body, so you can feel the change of the tide. In Rhinebeck the lake is a strong presence as well, its dimension is almost the same area as the plot, it is a back and forth. It emphasizes the different colors of the sky and of the trees, which change according to the seasons, and the reflection of them is almost more intense than the reflected element itself.

DC This in some way strengthens the perception of the time and the season of the year.

SH Yes, exactly. Every day is different and through these changes you have the perception of the cycle of time and of the seasons; this doesn't happen if you simply live isolated in the city. When I work in the Round Lake Hut I can feel that; this deep connection with the earth, but at the same time my mind is on the site of the projects. For example, this drawing is about a project competition for the New Shanghai Museum in China, it was made in the Hut but my mind was on the problems of Shanghai. This project idea rises from the dialectic between the poetic and the systematic. I thought of an old lecture by Karl Popper called "Clouds and Clocks". The clouds are the poetic object and the clocks are everything systematic, pragmatic, which correspond to the systematic grid office. Everything to do with this project is, once again, on only two sheets of paper and now there are ten people working on 16 boards and 3 models, but everything started here, on only these two sheets of paper.
Sometimes the first idea is not right and the time necessary to conceive a design depends on if you are satisfied with what you are doing. Not always do I

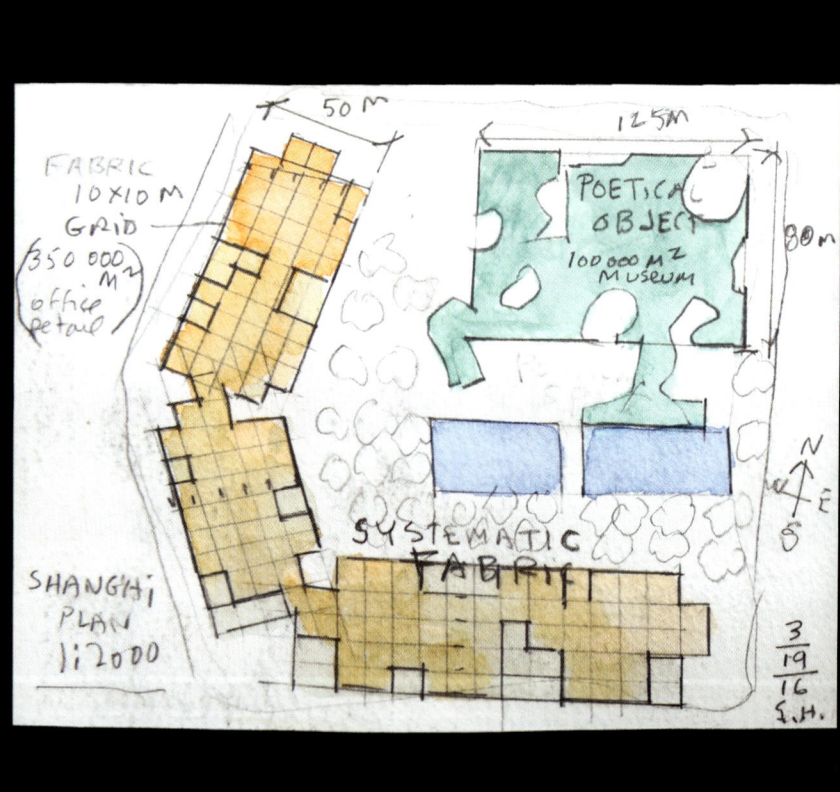

STUDY FOR SHANGHAI MUSEUM AND CBD BUILDING COMPETITION, 2016
STEVEN HOLL - WATERCOLOURS

MUSEUM → offices
100 000M² 350 000 M²

Poetic ← → SYSTEMATIC

CLOUDS ← CLOCKS

OBJECT ← → FABRIC

100 M

"POTS are fashioned
from clay but its
The Hollow That
MAKES A POT WORK"
TAO — LAO TZU

LIGHT
COURTS
CAST GLASS
RIBS

USEUM

EVELS

EDON
SMIC
DARK INTERIOR 125 M

3/19/16 S.H.

10 10 10 10 10 M

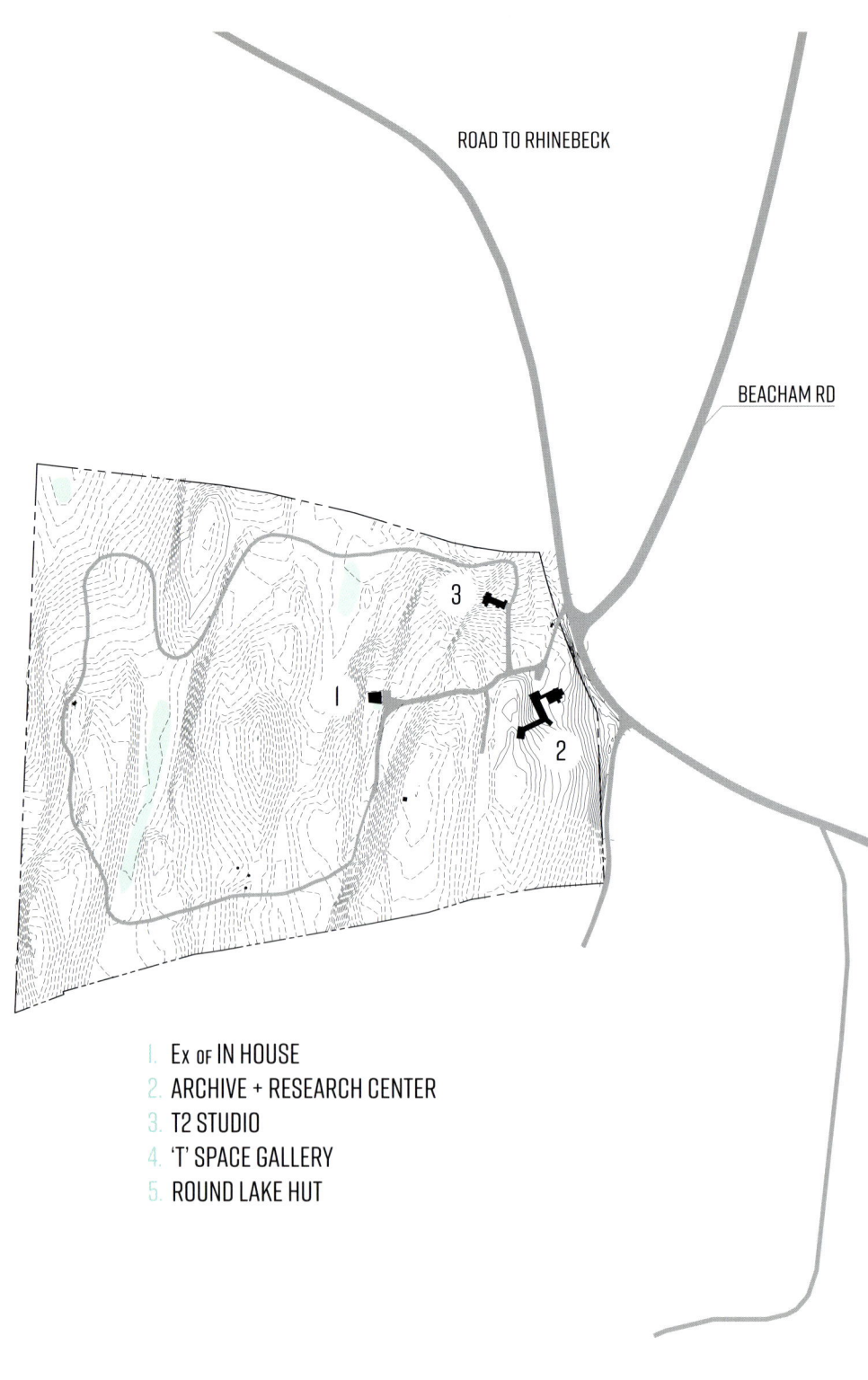

ROAD TO RHINEBECK

BEACHAM RD

1. Ex of IN HOUSE
2. ARCHIVE + RESEARCH CENTER
3. T2 STUDIO
4. 'T' SPACE GALLERY
5. ROUND LAKE HUT

ROUND POUND

5

4

ROUND LAKE RD

get it right at once, when I am not satisfied, after a critique, I start over again and I do another drawing and another scheme.

DC So this place is also crucial to meditate, to think and to find concentration.

SH Right, concentration; but I do also have ideas in other moments of the day and in different situations. You do not necessarily draw it out but it is certainly nice to be in that place (Round Lake Hut) and it is easier to work there.

DC Looking at the planimetry of the area, the Round Lake Hut seems to be part of a larger scale project.

SH Right, it is a project for 28 acres of land and it aims to preserve the natural land, acres and acres of natural land. In the planimetry you can see what is already there, such as the T-Space which was built five years ago and is now a gallery space. In the summer time, we have different kinds of shows: poetry, live music, architecture or painting or sculpture exhibitions and a large amount of people usually come on the occasion of these events.
Through the transformation of this old hunting shack, we have another gallery space and close to it there is one of the latest experimental projects of our office: Exploration of In. It is an artists' residency, some big installations sometimes take days to be prepared and then it could be a guest house for the artists. For example, last year, the sculptor Oscar Tuazon set up a big installation here and it took him a week's work on the site.

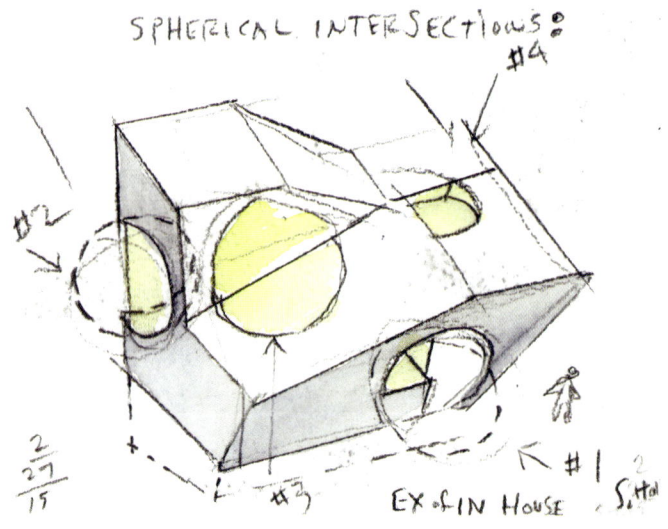

STUDY FOR EX OF IN HOUSE, STEVEN HOLL - WATERCOLOURS

DC I've read that this space is an experiment on the inner experience of the intersection of four spheres. It reflects too on the meaning of the space – on the inner and outer space, on what it contains and what does the containing.

SH Right, but I would also say "A compression". So the space comes from the intersection and compression of four spheres with a Tesseract and the house represents a sort of empty memory of the lake. Michael Bell calls this compression "A lake of the mind".

DC Thinking about these different buildings as a whole, the Round Lake Hut, we might say, represents the place where the ideas are created but it also belongs to the place where your architecture is constructed and experimented with. Could it be seen as a point of both departure and return – a continuous cycle – in your architectural work? We have talked about circularity, and in some way there is here too a form of return that could be reborn with the experimentation in your work.

SH Like the seasons, like the seasons come back in a continuous cycle. I have just been doing this lecture called "Time in architecture"; I identified nine types of time and I would like to say something about the duration of architecture and how we make buildings today, temporary and cheap buildings. I like instead to think about architecture as something that has a life and goes on. My project for the St. Ignatius chapel will be twenty years old in 2017 and it is still perfect, simply made out of concrete. I also like the idea that now in Princeton we are building the Lewis Center of Performing Arts using Lecce stone, right from town of

STUDY FOR EX OF IN HOUSE, STEVEN HOLL – WATERCOLOURS

7/5/55.H.

Lecce. The stone is 21 million years old, from a quarry that has been open for 2000 years, since Roman times. I find this time aspect in architecture interesting. I think about the Greeks and their circular perception of time, sequential, mythical, which allowed them to constantly make what they were building better and better, in a cyclical movement, and therefore, make them perfect in their architecture.

Nowadays time is linear, which is the opposite, and it creates the constant necessity of having something at the moment, a crazy linear time fashion, towards the next fashion and everything is going in a line, who knows where.

When I think about time I think about the cycle of the seasons. It is very important to live it. It is like a spiral and the cycle of seasons keeps you anchored and maybe it doesn't mean that it is going to be the same, or it is returning, but it is not going in a line like that either. This gives me a balance. Also, the idea of sequential, of mythical, is round; round, what else is round?! The moon, the womb of a mother is round. The community wherein we live and belong to, the family is round in a certain sense. We are on the earth, which is round and the planets as well, which operate in a kind of motion that is circular, so it is turning.

There are all these, let's say, dimensions of circularity that have to do also with the understanding of what an inward focus is. That is the reason why I like the metaphor that this Exploration of In House, of the four intersecting spheres, is like a "Lake of the mind", because that concerns a further compression toward something smaller, smaller and even smaller.

We could have built anything in there, right? But

I made this very small 918 square foot, but the feeling of the space isn't small when you go inside: everything is curved and spaced and then the intersection of the spheres. So yes, it is a "Cosa mentale". Architecture is "Una cosa mentale".

DC Is it a sort of centrifugal and centripetal force, is that right?

SH Yes, exactly.

DC How do you see this place developing in the future?

SH We want to preserve the natural landscape. It is a nature reserve. There is no intention of using the land as it happens with the suburban sprawl; it is just returning to nature. It is clear which part is occupied by humans and which one is all nature. It is a piece of land that was going to be divided into five suburban houses but we joined all the land again and we just put one tiny wooden house with these four intersecting spheres in the middle.
In 2002, I had an exhibition at the Basilica Palladiana, organized by Flavio Albanese and introduced by Francesco dal Co and it was about the edge of the city projects. On that occasion, I talked about the possibility of trying to make urban density, to eliminate the suburbs, to clean and replant the natural vegetation there.
The exhibition was prepared in order not to fill up the whole basilica, but to concentrate these urban projects just on one side of the space, and in the big open space left there was a tiny hut project, which we made for Richard Tuttle, called Turbulence House.

In a certain way this project is about preserving the landscape in the same polemic that the exhibition was in.

DC Looking carefully at your work reveals a sort of polarity between projects built in the countryside, which are restricted in size and "anchored" (cit.) in the natural context, and large urban projects, which are "anchored" (cit.) too in the place but are also directed towards the future development of the city on a larger, urban scale. It has been said before that sometimes the site of the work reflects something tied to the work itself. This seems to be reminiscent of your way of working – would you agree with that?

SH It is a similar thing. There are both in my work: high density projects in cities, with hybrid multifunctional buildings and singular buildings, isolated, in a different natural context. All the drawings, actually not all, but some of those projects in China were made here, in the Hut. So, in a way all my life is like that. The Horizontal Skyscraper project in Shenzhen – another high-density project – was made here in the Round Lake Hut and I love the absurdity of the scale shift and I also love the extreme craziness that you are seeing working a two-million-square foot horizontal skyscraper on a five-by-seven-inch pad.

DC What is your view of these two different directions in your work?

SH I love that. I truly believe in urbanism: projects on the edge of the cities, this notion of making the

city more habitable, hybrid buildings with multiple
functions and views and the possibility of a great
density. I think it is very important, like our Linked
Hybrid project in Beijing, with a water garden in the
center and the public spaces in the middle, it became
a kind of new urban space with all the different living
needs, cultural and educational functions, shopping,
working, culture spaces, cinema, and so on.
I believe that this is really important but at the
same time I also believe that preserving the natural
landscape is equally important. The human thought
process needs to connect itself to the cycle of nature
and of the seasons and therefore you cannot have a
complete life if you just live completely isolated in
the city. You need this connection to the land, it is a
spiritual thing.

THE INTERVIEW WAS GIVEN IN MAY 2010 AT THE STEVEN HOLL ARCHITECTS STUDIO IN NEW YORK CITY. ON THE SAME SUBJECT SEE ALSO THE TEXT BY STEVEN HOLL, MY HERMITAGE PUBLISHED IN DOMUS 1011, JULY-AUGUST 2010.

THE PURPOSE OF THIS PUBLICATION IS TO QUOTE, IN ITS ENTIRETY, THE TRANSCRIPT OF THE INTERVIEW MAINTAINING ITS SPONTANEITY IN A COMPLETELY UNABRIDGED FORMAT. WHAT FOLLOWS IS AN INFORMAL CONVERSATION WITH STEVEN HOLL ON INTUITION, PRAGMATISM AND CREATIVITY, ON DRAWING AS A FORM OF THOUGHT AND ON THE ROUND LAKE HUT, IN RHINEBECK.

TO BETTER UNDERSTAND AND CORRECTLY CONTEXTUALIZE WHAT WAS SAID A FINAL CHAPTER WILL DESCRIBE ONE OF STEVEN HOLL'S MOST RECENT PROJECTS, EX OF IN HOUSE, ALSO LOCATED IN RHINEBECK. AT THE TIME OF THE INTERVIEW THIS PROJECT HAD NOT BEEN BUILT ALTHOUGH NOW IT HAS BEEN COMPLETED.

EX OF IN HOUSE

The Ex of In House explores a language of space, aimed at inner spatial energy strongly bound to the ecology of the place - questioning current clichés of architectural language and commercial practice.
The house is a built manifestation of the research and development project Explorations of "IN" under development at Steven Holl Architects since June 2014.

SEVEN POINT MANIFESTO FOR EXPLORATIONS OF "IN"

1. TO STUDY ARCHITECTURE FREED FROM THE PURELY OBJECTIVE

2. FROM ORIGINS OF ARCHITECTURE WE EXPLORE "IN"

3. "IN": ALL SPACE IS SACRED SPACE

4. THE ARCHITECTURE OF "IN" DOMINATES SPACE VIA SPACE

5. INTRINSIC "IN" IS AN ELEMENTAL FORCE OF SENSUAL BEAUTY

6. "IN" IS USELESS, BUT IN THE FUTURE IT WILL BE USED. PURPOSE FINDS "IN"

7. THE THING CONTAINING IS NOT THE THING CONTAINED

On twenty-eight acres of a forested rock outcropping, the site named 'T2 reserve' has been established as an experimental topological landscape. Slated to be a subdivision with five suburban house plots, the site was joined into one natural preserved landscape.

As a compressed form of 918 square feet on a site of twenty-eight preserved rural acres, the house serves as an alternative to modernist suburban houses that "sprawl in the landscape". Instead, the Ex of In is a house of compression and inner voids.

The house's geometry is formed from spherical spaces intersecting with Tesseract trapezoids intended as a catalyst of volumetric inner space. The geometry of the spherical intersections begins to be felt at the entry porch; an orb of wood carved out of the house volume welcomes the entrant.

The shift in section of the house alters internal space with a vertical dynamic spatial overlap. Situated around one main volume, open to the second level, with the kitchen placed in the center, alternative use patterns are created. There are zero bedrooms, yet the house can sleep five.

Instead of fossil fuel, the house is heated geothermally. Instead of grid power, the house has electricity from the sun. Thin film SoloPower photovoltaic cells are connected to a Sonnen battery energy storage system, allowing the house to be energy independent.

All light fixtures are 3D printed in PLA corn-starch-based bioplastic. Glass and wood are locally sourced.

The house was made almost entirely from raw materials by the builders, crafting solid mahogany window and door frames, a mahogany stair and birch plywood walls.

There is no use of sheetrock. The spherical intersection space was also crafted in curved, thin wood layers. All-natural oiled wood and plywood interior finishes are part of the arte povera materiality and economy of this place of wabi-sabi.

FACT SHEET

PROGRAM: GUEST HOUSE / ARTIST RESIDENCE

ESTIMATED DATE OF COMPLETION: JULY 2016

SITE AREA: 918 SQ FT

BUILT AREA: 28 ACRES

MATERIALS: WOOD CONSTRUCTION, CNC CARVED WOOD DETAILS, THIN FILM SOLAR PANELS, RECYCLED GLASS EXTERIOR

CREDIT SHEET

TEAM: STEVEN HOLL ARCHITECTS, STEVEN HOLL (DESIGN ARCHITECT), DIMITRA TSACHRELIA (DESIGN ARCHITECT, PROJECT ARCHITECT), YULIYA SAVELYEVA, MICHAEL HADDY (PROJECT TEAM), RUOYU WEI (ASSISTANT PROJECT ARCHITECT)

INGEGNERE STRUTTURALE: ROBERT SILMAN ASSOCIATES

CLIMATE ENGINEERS: TRANSSOLAR

IMPRESA: JPL HOME IMPROVEMENT, JAVIER GOMEZ

EAST ELEVATION

"CLOSE TO THE PULSE OF THE SKY," THE EX OF IN HOUSE FACES THE RISING SUN WITH THE ENTRY SPACE FACING TOWARD THE COMING OF THE DAWN LIGHT EACH MORNING.
THE FORWARD LEANING FAÇADE SLICES AN INTERSECTING SPHERICAL VOLUME EMBRACING THE VISITOR IN A WOMB-LIKE WELCOMING.

SOUTH ELEVATION

THE SOUTH ELEVATION INTERSECTS THE CYCLIC ENERGY OF THE SUN VIA A ROUND CUT, LARGE ENOUGH TO SUN-HEAT THE LIVING SPACE IN WINTER WITH A SHADE DEPLOYED IN SUMMER.

WEST ELEVATION

THE WEST ELEVATION IS CUT BY A REMOVED
SPHERICAL THREE-WAY INTERSECT IN GLASS
THAT INCLUDES A GLASS FLOOR. THE EVERYDAY
MIRACLE OF A HUDSON VALLEY SUNSET-WITH ITS
DISTANT CHANGING GLOW THAT SO INSPIRED THE
HUDSON RIVER SCHOOL PAINTERS-IS ENCIRCLED
WEST, PARTLY SOUTH, AND DOWN THROUGH THE
GLASS FLOOR.

NORTH ELEVATION

THE NORTH ELEVATION WILL ALSO GLOW AT FIRST
LIGHT OF SUNRISE AS THE CURVED SLICE OF THE
SPHERICAL ENTRY BOUNCES LIGHT TO THE NORTH.

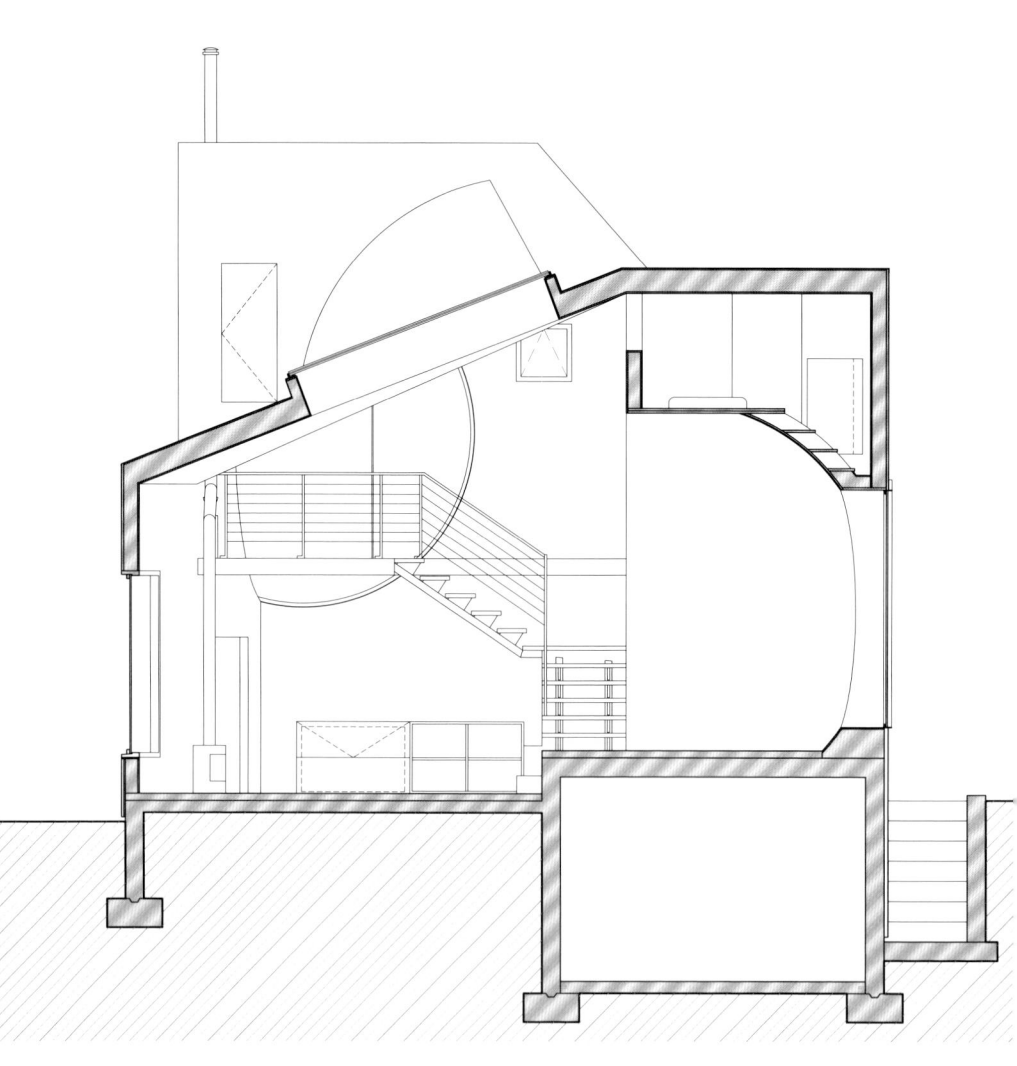

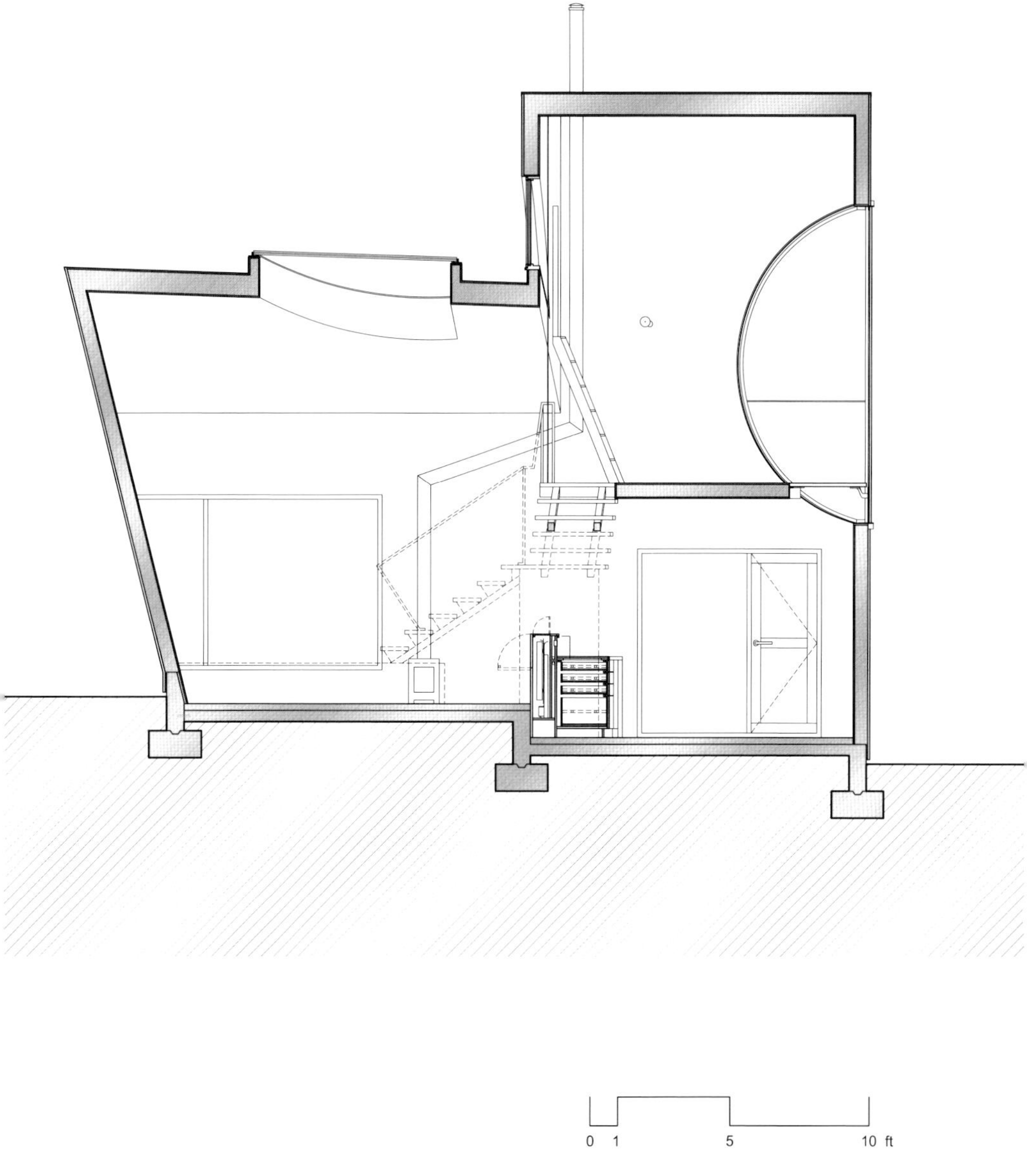

0 1   5   10 ft

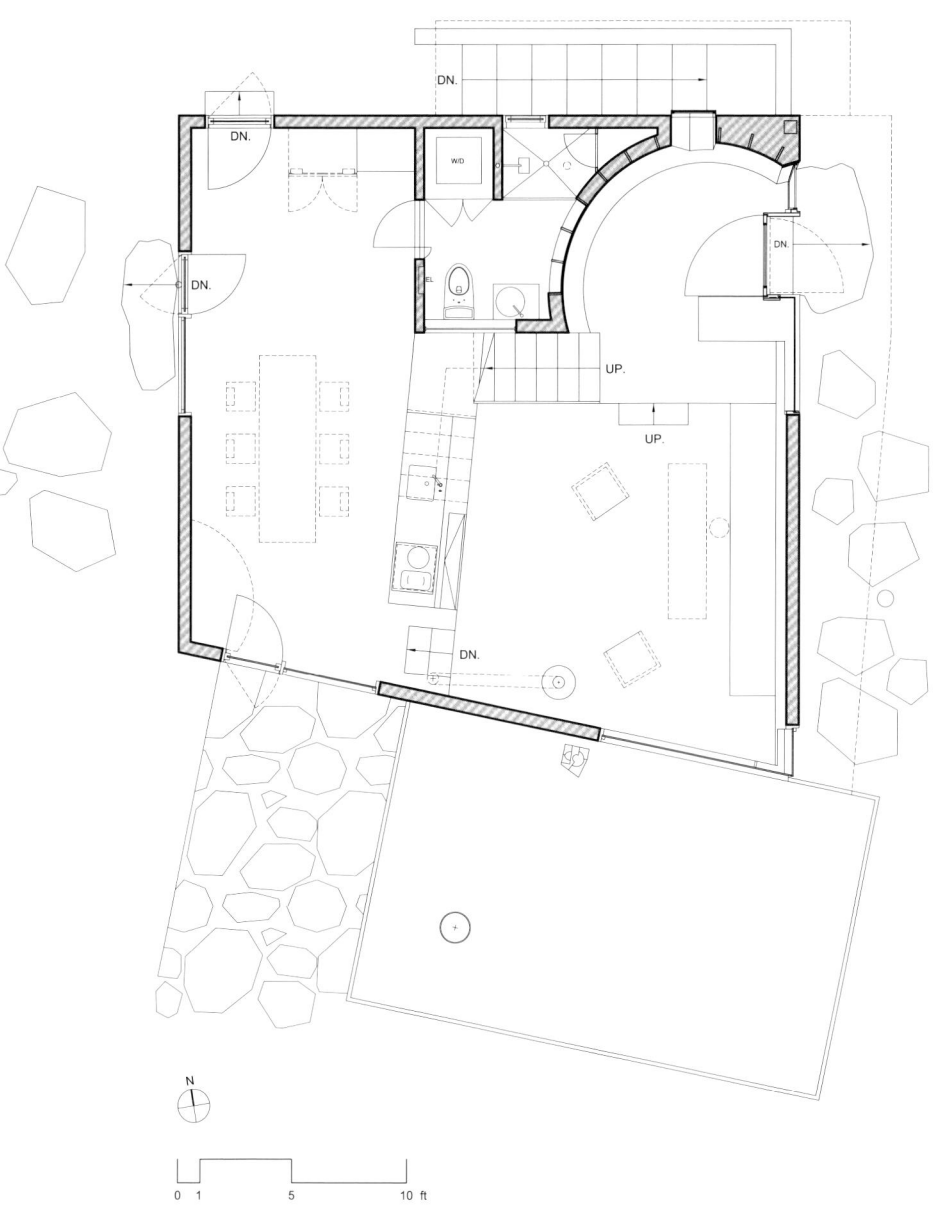

DN.

DN.

DN.

W/D

DN.

UP.

UP.

EL

DN.

N

0 1   5   10 ft

DIANA CARTA

CONCLUSION

There is no such thing as architecture. There is the spirit of architecture, but it has no presence. What does have presence is a work of architecture. At best it must be considered as an offering to architecture itself, merely because of the wonder of its beginning.

Louis I.Kahn

VENN DIAGRAMS:

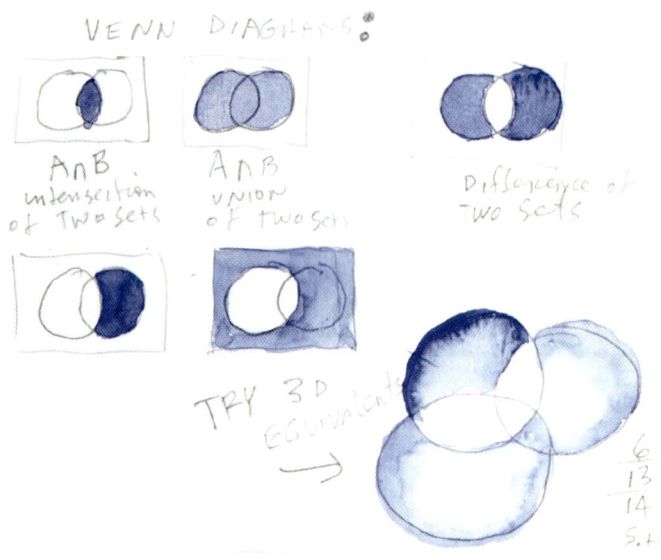

A∩B
intersection
of two sets

A∩B
union
of two sets

Difference of
two sets

TRY 3D
EQUIVALENT →

6
13
14
S.+

EXPLORATIONS of "IN"
A) SPHERICS SECTIONS →
B) TRAPAZOIDAL SECTIONS

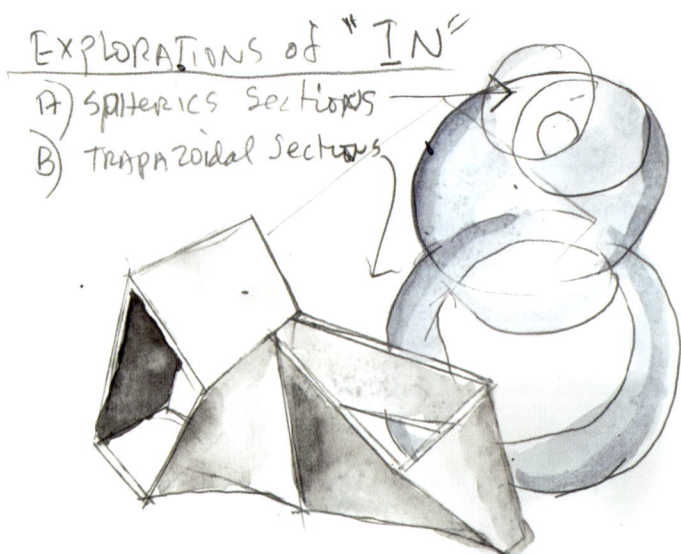

Exploration of In is a project which rises from the interest, referred to as almost an "obsession" by Steven Holl, in light and inner space. Architecture is not only understood and interpreted as an object conceived from the outside, but rather it focuses the attention toward the inside, what he considers the "transformative space". The research, or better "exploration", becomes a sort of path for architecture and at the same time it is an invitation to be more willing to face design in these terms. The Exploration of In project, therefore, starts with a work on the subjects of space and abstraction, revealing links between architecture and neuroscience, of which nobody had ever spoken before and this is an exemplifying confirmation of one's continuous need for abstraction.

ARCHITECTURE IS NOT ONLY UNDERSTOOD AND INTERPRETED AS AN OBJECT CONCEIVED FROM THE OUTSIDE, BUT RATHER IT FOCUSES THE ATTENTION TOWARD THE INSIDE

Following the different phases of the work, the project starts with the elaboration of Venn Diagrams and further modifications, which from the beginning were always drawn. Furthermore, for each phase a 3D printed model was created.
The first step consisted in the elaboration of Venn diagrams of spheres and intersecting spheres (first model, image on the following page).
Once a representative physical model of that phase had been realized, it was decided to do a reverse: its reverse; a sort of negative. However, the inversion starts from the inner space, it is a spatial inversion of what is contained; looking at the interior and not at the "object" (second model, image on the following page).
The next step consisted of the intersection between

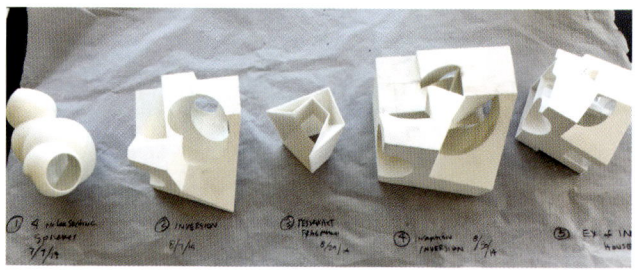

what had been obtained up to then with a Tesseract, arriving at a "fragment" of Tesseract (third model) which in turn was inserted into the four intersecting reversed spheres, obtained during the first phase (fourth model). A final step then brought everything together, almost spontaneously, into the realization of a project for a small house, or rather a guest house (fifth model).

When entering the space, you do not need to know all the research that has taken place to understand its geometry because, through the different sphericities, the space engages the visitor in a total experience: on a physical, mental and spiritual level.
As such, a spatial energy is created which is emphasized by the light reflecting off the internal spherical surfaces at each moment of the day, which in turn creates evolving forms of light that move throughout the internal space and different levels.
During the end of the research and the study of Exploration of In, an opportunity presented itself to purchase a plot of land of 11 hectares in Rhinebeck, which had just been put up for sale. It was decided that this land, which was supposed to be divided into five plots for five suburban houses respectively, should become part of

one entire nature reserve, in the center of which the Ex of
In House was built.

It is completely handmade and the internal curved
surfaces were sanded like those of a resonating chamber
of a musical instrument.

Every aspect of the project was conceived to have a
completely energy-efficient house with no energy
consumption.

This house, moreover, stands for all the arguments
of form versus content. The project focuses on the
connection between the form and what is contained
inside, in other words, the function. Through the
development of the idea of "exploration", a result where
all the different spaces work seamlessly and spontaneously together has been achieved. The fact that the house does not have any bedrooms is noteworthy, since it is a usual characterizing

IT IS COMPLETELY HANDMADE
AND THE INTERNAL CURVED
SURFACES WERE SANDED
LIKE THOSE OF A RESONATING
CHAMBER OF A MUSICAL
INSTRUMENT

aspect of the entity of a residential project. Here, there
are none, but the spatial organization provides five
places for sleeping. Everything works as a purpose (point
6 of the Manifesto: "IN" is useless, but in the future it will
be used. Purpose finds "IN").

According to Steven Holl "Architecture can change your
life and can change the way you live life, the way you can
see, the way you can feel" and quoting Winston Churchill
– We shape our buildings and thereafter they shape us –
he then adds "I think this house has that shaping ability
and where does it come from? It doesn't come from
functions, it comes from a spatial energy".

Printed in Italy
September 2018